TIPS TO INCREASE YOUR WEALTH, HEALTH AND LIFE

BY JON ROBERT QUINN

Introduction

Your Job

What is Organization?

Starting Your First Business

Building My First Retail Store

Building a Foundation

Personal Finance

Spenders, Savers and Investors

Stocks

Using OPM

Encouraging Entrepreneurship

Be a Leader

Be Original

Building a Business System

Expect Good Things

Increase Sales by Properly Training Sales People

Happiness

Conclusion

Introduction

Hello, I am Jon Robert Quinn, a business owner, investor and musician. In this book, I will talk to you about ways I have used to increase my Wealth, Health and Life. I'm not going to tell you how to get rich quick, rather I will show you ways I have used to get rid of my boring, go nowhere job, start businesses and build a path to financial wealth. I will show you ways on how to get your finances in order and use the investment vehicles available. Sit back and listen to these lessons and think about ways you can apply these lessons into your life. Only YOU can decide your fate to your future.

Your Job

Most people hate their job. A lot of people love their job. And it's those people who have done their homework and found something that works for them. If you're ready to get rid of your JOB and start a business, whether it's working from home or opening a restaurant, then listen up.

You get up every morning and think "why do I go to work?" Well, it's simple! You must eat. You must feed your family. You must live somewhere and you want nice things. So, you put up with it. Every single day. What if it could be different? You're probably thinking to yourself, I don't have time. Whether you're young or old, have a family or not, there is time to start a business or do something that YOU want to do.

You need to start with you. It's called organization. You need to organize your life to increase your productivity, finance and health. I will talk about organization throughout this audio book.

I remember when I was working at Office Max for minimum wage. I was working 8 hours a day on my feet and literally taking home something like $1200.00 per month. It was crazy. I remember my boss telling me that she had never used a resume to get a job. Maybe that's why she was in her mid-forties and working in customer service. I knew this wasn't what I wanted to do. I wanted to play music. I wanted to tour. I wanted to write records and become somebody.

One day I came into work and one of my co-workers said "hey, I saw you were showcased on Bearshare. I heard your music. Not bad." That was a huge accomplishment for me. This was an international website that showcased musicians from around the world. I knew about being showcased on the site, but never thought in a million years that a co-worker of mine at Office Max would see me online, listen to my music and acknowledge me as a musician. I knew at that point what I needed to be doing.

Immediately, I started booking shows at every venue I could. It didn't matter if it was local or out of town, for pay or for free. I knew I needed to be playing and producing and performing my music. I remember filling out so many time off requests that the little box on my boss' office door was over flowing with days I couldn't work because I was playing shows somewhere and couldn't work. She came up to me one day and said, "you're going to have to decide whether you're going to work here or play music. You can't do both." I chose music and never looked back.

This is a prime example of figuring out what you want to do and doing it. We all have something special inside of us. What are you passionate about?

What is organization?

Organization is nothing more than putting something in its place. For instance, let's start with something we all have, a closet. Start by putting your pants on one side and your shirts on the other side. Your socks will go in one drawer and underwear in another drawer. That's it! Really that's all it takes.

So, when I talk to you about getting out of your dead-end job, you need to start by organizing your time. It's your time and you need some of it for you!

I hear a lot of people with excuses, "I don't have time for this or time for that", but you need to think about what it is YOU need for YOU to be happy.

So, you get up in the morning, get the kids ready, go to work, come home, feed the kids, bathe them, get them in bed and you're tired. You follow this routine for years and years and never leave that dead-end job. So, try this! When you get home and your TV is on, get a piece of paper and make a list as long as you want of the things you would love to do for a living. Don't be foolish and say an astronaut. Though it can happen, that takes decades of training.

After you have created your list, check off the ones that don't really interest you. This is where you decide on what it is you want to do. Do you want to work in medical? Or law enforcement? What about clothing and fashion? Maybe photography? Or do you really love purses? Or fixing things? Every day start putting a little time, maybe just a half hour a day into that goal. As you become more involved in it, you put more time into it. Get the kids involved. If they enjoy it, you increase your productivity and are spending more time with the family.

So, let's say you chose medical. There are plenty of online classes that work around your schedule and in a couple years, you'll have a degree to help get a job that you'd like.

Let say you wanted to start a business. In the back of your mind, you have always wanted to design clothing. You need to start by finding out what it is you want to do. That's not my job, that's your job. Then you need to DO. Start with making just a few pieces at a time. The kids will probably help you because when the clothes are done, they will probably want to wear them to school. Then their friends will see the new threads and want some too. As popularity builds, you start attending local trade shows and festivals. Usually those events are on weekends, so you don't have to take much time from work. All it takes is organization.

Starting Your First Business

Starting a business is easy. And depending on what it is you want to start, it's fairly inexpensive. Small business loans are available if you want to open a small restaurant and investors love to get involved in new projects when presented to them. That's what they do, invest.

Now, I'm not saying anybody can start a business, because they cannot. It takes passion, determination, a lot of patience and a lot of hard work. Even though its hard work, it doesn't seem like it if you're enjoying what you do. So, how do you start your first business?

Here's an example.

You love purses. You walk into a store, see a cute purse and go OOOH, I want that. And usually you end up buying it. There are two ways to look at this? You work for somebody else, hate your job, but you're shopping for purses. Let's use that time and turn play into business. Let's say, you have no kids. You come home from work and plop down in front of the TV and your boyfriend comes over for dinner. A little snuggle snuggle. He goes home and goes to bed. That time could've been put to good use.

Companies all over the world sell purses. Designer brands and no-name brands. Find a distributor that sells purses. You can do this by looking up Purse Distributors in a search engine. Call them up and ask them for a dealer application. Most likely you will need a business license and sellers permit before creating an account as a dealer with that distributor. Go to your local City Hall for the business license. It shouldn't cost you any more than sixty dollars. The seller permit you can get from your Board of Equalization office. They usually don't cost anything. Once you get your permits, fill out the dealer application, send it to the distributor and viola. You're now a dealer. Now it's time to sell. Start small. Buy two or three to make sure the quality is there first. You don't want to sell junk to your customers. You'll make a couple of bucks, but they won't come back to buy anything else. When the product arrives, if you're happy with the quality, show it to your friends. You may sell a few or even more to your friends and family. When you have decided that you're 1) having fun and 2) making money, it's time to make a larger purchase.

Before you go any further make sure you're organized. You need a place to work. Do you have a place you can work and keep track of receipts, invoices and expenses? You need a small desk in the corner of your home that you can work and actually get things done.

You need to separate expenses from sales invoices and so on. Pick up a small business software package from your local office supply store or you can do what I did and build your own.

If you put an hour a day into the business, after a couple of months you'll see a steady increase in sales if you build a solid foundation. I will talk to you about that shortly.

So, you just got home from work and there is a big box on your porch that contains twenty-four purses. You can't wait to open it. What are you going to do with all those purses? That's easy! Sell them. Flea Markets, online classified ads and many other avenues are ways YOU can sell that product. Remember, the faster you sell them, the more money that goes into your pocket and quicker you can order more purses. You now own a business. Congratulations.

Building My First Retail Store

I remember sitting at home one night and getting the crazy idea of opening a retail store. I already had dozens of online stores selling motorcycle gear and my apartment literally had hundreds of items I would be taking to local flea markets and selling on Craigslist. I literally have two to three people per day coming by my home pick up gear, so a retail store was inevitable.

The first challenge was getting the capital needed and finding a good store front. Retail space is very expensive and the last thing we want to do is go out of business before we are actually in business. I scoured craigslist looking at retail space and the cheapest place I could find was about eight hundred square feet and about one thousand two hundred dollars per month.

Building a retail store, you need to pay attention to ROI (return on investment). ROI is simple. If you invest one thousand two hundred dollars per month into a space, the space must create a return equal or greater to your cost of the space. My recommendation is two-to-one. Meaning, if you spend one thousand two hundred dollars per month, the space should create a return of two thousand four hundred dollars per month net or after expenses.

My decision was instead of opening a retail store, I would rent some commercial office space for under four hundred dollars per month. The space was much smaller and in a strip mall, which was harder to find and less retail looking, but my return would cover the expenses of rent, electricity, internet, phone, etc. This was a smart move and an instant success for my customers. Several other stores would soon follow.

Building retail stores was a challenge, but a fun challenge. I want to use the space below to show you how to properly design and build your business structure. It's all about leveraging your money and guaranteeing a return.

Product A: Cost $2.00 Retail $9.99 Profit $7.99
Product B: Cost $10.00 Retail $29.99 Profit $19.99
Product C: Cost $20.00 Retail $49.99 Profit $29.99
Product D: Cost $40.00 Retail $79.99 Profit $39.99
Product E: Cost $50.00 Retail $99.99 Profit $49.99
Product F: Cost $90.00 Retail $179.99 Profit $89.99

Above you see a variety of products with our unit cost, retail price and profit. Now a couple things I want to point out. Sales will obviously affect your profit margins, as well as theft, as well as taxes paid to IRS. You also have to factor in the cost of doing business, ie: Employees, Rent, etc, but this is a general idea.

Now obviously it makes sense to sell the more expensive item because you'll make more money on that item. However, not every customer wants to spend hundreds of dollars during one purchase. So, those clients will want a product of maybe a little lesser quality but something that will fit their budget. Now flipping the coin. There are customers who absolutely want the more expensive product and will pay full retail for it.

There are three types of customers. I call them the Dollar Store Customer, The Wal Mart Customer and The Nordstrom Customer. All three customers are shoppers and buyers in your store, however their wants and needs are different. The Dollar Store customer doesn't make a ton of money and wants whatever will get the job done for as little money as possible. The Wal Mart Customer wants a good product, not superior and wants it for a fair price. They won't buy the cheapest product but also aren't interested in the top of the line either. The Nordstrom customer may make the same money as The Wal Mart Customer but will take their time and buy the best they can get because they feel like they deserve it. Some Nordstrom customers make more money than The Wal Mart shopper and simply don't care about price. What does all this mean?

When pricing your products and building your store, make sure you have products available each of those customers. You want all of them in your store. However, when that Nordstrom customer is buying your product, this is a fantastic time to upsell them with VALUE, meaning, you can sell them an additional product or products of lesser quality and they feel like they are getting more for less. This also works with your Wal Mart customers with small ten dollar add ones. By showing the benefits of accessories, both The Wal Mart and Nordstrom customer will most likely spend more on additional products. This increases your point of sale transaction amount increasing the health of your business.

The following exercise will determine what type of client your business will be geared towards.

Building a Foundation

As I said before, building a business is easy, but it takes time. To build a successful business, you need to build a foundation, also called a business system. This system is in place to ensure that every transaction goes smoothly and accurately. Without a system, the business will fail.

The system starts before you make your first sale. It starts with how you invoice your customer, how you enter the sale into your database and how you file the invoice after the sale is complete. Also, you need to keep track of expenses. A lot of people say it is okay to lose money your first year in business. I think that is all wrong. If you are already losing money your first year in business, then your system you have in place is failing you. If you lose money your first year in business, how will you survive five or ten or even fifteen years later? You can't.

Here's an example of how it should work. You order one dozen pair of sunglasses. The sunglasses cost you two dollars each. You want to sell them for ten dollars each. Ideally, you have a profit of eight dollars per pair, but no, you do not. Factor in shipping from the vendor to you. That was six dollars for the dozen, equaling out to fifty cents per pair. Your profit is now seven dollars fifty cents per pair. Remember, you still must pay for invoices, advertising, and a place to sell your sunglasses. If you are selling at the local flea market, then you need to factor in the expenses of the space you will be renting at the flea market. So, obviously if you take a dozen pair of sunglasses to the flea market, you will be losing money. But what if you took twenty dozen sunglasses to the flea market? Let's look at the figures.

With one dozen pair of sunglasses. Your cost is two dollars each. You sell all twelve pair at ten dollars each and take home one hundred-twenty dollars. Your cost plus shipping for the sunglasses were thirty dollars, the space rental was forty dollars and an invoice book is two dollars. After all was said and done, before taxes, you made forty-eight dollars. Not bad from money for a dozen pair of sunglasses.

Now let's get realistic. Nobody goes to the flea market with one dozen pair of sunglasses. More like twenty dozen sunglasses. And typically, sunglasses sell for about five dollars a pair at the flea market. So, let's look at the figures. Twenty dozen sunglasses at two dollars each will cost you four hundred eighty dollars. Shipping will be a little cheaper because of the quantity. Add about twelve dollars for shipping. You're at four hundred ninety-two dollars. You will need tables to display your products. That's about one hundred dollars. You're now at five hundred ninety-two dollars. Space rental at the flea market is forty dollars. Now you're at 632.00. The numbers add up quickly. Now let's start selling and have some fun. Now you probably won't sell every pair of sunglasses in one day, but let's say you did. After selling two hundred forty pair of sunglasses, you will have earned one thousand two hundred dollars. Now subtract your expenses of six hundred thirty-two dollars. Before taxes, you will have earned five hundred sixty-eight dollars. Not bad for a day's work. Take that money and buy more glasses. But remember, you only have to buy those tables once, so next time, one hundred more dollars will be in your pocket.

You don't have to only sell sunglasses. This was nothing more than an example. Whatever it is that you like, there is a market for it and you can make money selling the things that you love. I like music, so I write music, record it and sell it. I love motorcycles, so I sell motorcycle helmets and accessories. I love cars, so I sell auto parts. Not only have I been selling at flea markets for years, I also travel to fairs and festivals, motorcycle and automotive events as well as online. I own dozens of websites that sell thousands of items each and every month. I enjoy what I do and continue to wake up every day working in an industry I love.

Personal Finance

Before you can start your first business, you need to get your personal finances in order. Balancing a checkbook is the very beginning. Being able to balance a checkbook is not easy if you have never done it, it takes practice. Like riding a bike. Once you get the hang of it, you can get creative to build personal wealth.

I have eleven banks. I started with one like everybody else and built to two and so on. I have several savings accounts and every account plays a different role. Whether it's for paying bills or saving money for something I want to buy or just putting away for my future. That money is there for protection. Money is power and without it, you're weak. Without money, we cannot eat or survive. So why live paycheck to paycheck? What if something breaks on your car? Are you going to use credit cards? I'm not. I have money put away just for that reason, IF something comes up.

Here's how to get started. Most of us already have a bank account. Get used to documenting EVERY SINGLE entry in and out of the account using Excel from Microsoft. If you don't have Excel, there are other Spreadsheet software programs available.

You start with your current balance. Every time you purchase something, take the receipt, put it into your wallet, NOT the bottom of your purse and when you get home enter it into your spreadsheet. Every night before you go to bed, you will know where every cent is going. Remember, organization. Most banks now have Online Banking. Online Banking is NOT ENOUGH to be organized. Take the extra step by creating a Spreadsheet. This makes things so much easier. Each night, make sure you have lined up every transaction with your online banking, make sure you enter the receipts that have not yet cleared, such as pending checks and restaurant receipts. When you get up, those uncleared transactions may have now cleared so again line up your online banking with your spreadsheet. You will at every moment's notice know every cent you have spent and know to the penny how much money is available in your account.

Now, let's start building wealth. If you don't already have a savings account, open one. Here's why. We are going to use your online banking as a tool to build wealth. Call or visit your bank and set up an automatic transfer program that will transfer a small amount of money from your checking account into your saving account on a regular basis. Let's start small, like five dollars a day. If you can do more, great!

If five dollars was pulled from your checking Monday thru Friday and placed into your savings, in one week, you would have saved twenty-five dollars. It may not seem like a lot. But here is where it gets fun. In only one month, you have saved approximately one hundred dollars. In a year, that is one thousand two hundred dollars. If you can transfer more each day, do it. Remember to pay yourself first. If you put that money into savings each day, you will find you have less money to spend on things like coffee and snacks from the vending machines at work.

So, if you apply both lesson one, starting your first business and lesson two, saving, think of all the extra money you will have. Just because you have extra money, it doesn't mean you need to spend it. As your savings grows, the interest the account accrues will increase. The more you make, the more you save.

Spenders, Savers and Investors

There are 3 types of people in this world. Spenders, Savers and Investors.

Spenders spend every cent they get, whether it's on newspapers or coffee at work. If they have it, they spend it. That is the absolute worst habit you can have. Savers save as much as they can and prefer not to use investment vehicles. Investors, save and spend. They spend on what they need. Then use the difference to save and invest in vehicles that will over time make them even more money. Stocks are a great vehicle to invest in. Many people say stocks are a risky investment, but so is spending every penny you get without a rhyme or reason.

Stocks

Stocks are a very fun and interactive way to build wealth that is yes risky, but only risky if you don't understand how the numbers works. There is a time and place for everything. So, how do you know when the time is right? Study the trends. Look at a company's history. Read the news. Look at products that companies are building for release in the near future. You must believe in the company before you buy a stock. If you do not, then how do you expect to make money if you yourself do not believe in the company.

You like cars. In 2009 the auto industry changed dramatically. Companies that had been around for one hundred years filed for bankruptcy. So, I'll ask you again. When is a good time to buy? As soon as that company pulls out of bankruptcy. The stock will be low. Buy it. Don't spend your savings. Only buy what you are comfortable buying. Remember that the broker will take it's share. It's usually a flat rate fee of about ten dollars per purchase. Buying or selling is called a trade. Remember, when you sell that stock or shares of that stock, they will charge you that same fee. As the market grows and demand increases on that stock, the price goes up.

It's a very simple formula. Demand goes up, price goes up. This formula follows us everywhere we go, whether it's the fuel pump or bread at the grocery store.

So, when you're looking for that first stock, consider companies that are strong. Here's an example. Company XYZ has been in business for one hundred years. Their stock is currently twenty-five dollars per share. At ten shares, you will pay two hundred fifty dollars, plus the broker fee. We'll say it's ten dollars. So, you would pay two hundred sixty dollars for ten shares. With the fees included, you paid twenty-six dollars per share. This company has a new gadget coming out that the magazines and review companies are saying will be a big hit, such as the iPod, palm pilot, LCD tv, etc. Demand on these new products will drive the price of the stock up. That's what you want to look for. Three weeks after you bought your stock, the new product comes out and demand drives the stock to thirty dollars per share. Your stock, minus your fees has put forty dollars in your pocket. That's good. That's money. Congratulations, you just made money in the stock market. Now find your next stock. We will go back to cars. During the recession in 2009, people were afraid of buying stocks in the auto industry. I made most of my money in stocks during the 2009 recession purchasing stocks in the auto industry. There are a lot of companies in this industry other than manufacturers. There are dealership chains, rental car companies, maintenance and repair companies. These companies were thriving during this time. I bought a fair amount of stock in each company and sat back and watched the stocks grow. People have to drive cars and whether they are buying new cars or used cars, they also have to rent cars when they travel and have to maintain their cars, so they will last. Also look at computer companies.

As our world gets further out of the industrial age and into the information age, communications companies will grow. Websites and media companies are making more money now than they ever have and these are also very good companies to consider. Remember to look at the trends and have faith in what it is the company is doing before you buy.

Using OPM

After you have created a nice stock portfolio, you can use OPM (Other People's Money) to your advantage. Let's say you spent a total of five hundred dollars in stocks and your stock is currently worth one thousand dollars. You can sell five hundred of those shares to purchase more stock from either this company or another company. Those shares can make you even more money as the market grows.

When I was building The Good Life Show with Jon Robert Quinn, I had just been laid off from my job as a mortgage loan officer. See, I have a problem working for people. When I don't like something, I speak my mind. My clients know it and respect me for it. But, when you walk into your boss' office and speak your mind, you get to go home early and get paid early too. The problem is, you never get to come back.

Back to my story. Where was I? Oh yes, OPM. I had no money to invest into the creation of The Good Life Show. However, I had value. See, money is nothing more than the exchange of value for value. Meaning, when you have something to offer somebody, you can get what you want equaling the value. So, when I was approached to do a talk show, it was very expensive to create, and I was literally a couple days from just getting canned by the mortgage company. I knew however that I had something other people needed.

The radio station need a thousand dollars per month for air time and I needed to survive. All I did was create value. I would approach businesses and sell them sponsor air time for five-hundred dollars per month. We could literally fit a half a dozen of these spots in a show and create thousands of dollars of passive income by giving them affordable air-time broadcasting their businesses to the community via the radio.

Within three weeks of being laid off or fired, whatever you want to call it, I was on the air, fully funded with sustainable income. Fast forward a year and The Good Life Show with Jon Robert Quinn was literally the number one show in Sacramento, California because we were providing valued to our clients.

To this day, I have never spent one penny of my own money on The Good Life Show. That folks is what you call OPM.

Encouraging Entrepreneurship

Running a business is different than being an entrepreneur. An Entrepreneur takes opportunities and thrives on them. He or she can literally take any situation and capitalize from it. A business owner basically takes a product or service and either makes a living with it or works part-time as a hobby. An Entrepreneur owns and has built many businesses and is well diversified in a variety of markets. A business owner plays it safe and works hard for his or her money. An entrepreneur takes calculated risks and works hard making sure his or her money is working hard for them. Personal wealth and growth flow around an entrepreneur. The passion, determination and drive for success is what makes an entrepreneur an entrepreneur. In order to be an entrepreneur, you must get creative, remove yourself from the box and get yourself ready for the ride of your life.

Be A Leader

When building a business, being a leader is most important, with the exception of finances of course. When you're a leader, the employees and customers will respect you better than if you're a cool guy. Whatever you do, do not be a push over. Being a leader doesn't mean you should boss people around, but you must be a boss. You must be there as a mentor for your employees as well as love and respect each customer. If you're a micro manager, you will irritate your employees and lose respect. If you're a bully, not only will you upset your employees, but it will bleed on to your customers, in turn tarnishing the culture your business brings and the company reputation.

So, how do you become a leader without being a jerk? It starts with being respectful to your employees and understanding their needs, but also having good policies in place. Give people the benefit of the doubt but don't let them take advantage. Take interest in them. Get to know their families, their kids. For customers, giving a little freebee when it's within a few days of their birthday may cut into your bottom end, but will do wonders to repeat business, keeping you in business and increasing word of mouth advertising. For your employees, on their birthday, giving a fifty-dollar gift card for a night out on the town and have them take the day off. This will do wonders to the loyalty they have for the company. When they return to work, they will actually enjoy the atmosphere and in turn will probably work a little harder. However, when they do wrong, show them what they did wrong and teach them the right way to get it done. If they keep making the same mistake over and over, maybe this isn't the best place for them.

When they need help or have a question, sit down

and talk them through it. Show them that their hard work is appreciated. The best advice I can give is this, look at every boss you've worked for. Write down what you liked and didn't like and make sure you provide your employees with what it was your past employers were lacking. Company growth starts from the top and rolls downhill. If you treat people right and set the expectation, that behavior follows all the way down the chain with the result being the customer. Happier employees mean happier customers.

Be Original

For your company to be successful, you must be original. You must think differently and open your mind to change. Being original entails thinking of new creative ways to accomplish challenges and building structure.

Originality means taking your craziest and wildest ideas and finding ways to make them work using your skills and tools.

Justin Bieber was original when it came to his hairstyle. Baskin Robbins was original by offering thirty-one flavors. Dodge was original by offering the Hemi. How are you or can you be different? When designing your business model, set yourself apart from the competition.

Step One: Your product or service. Has anybody done it before you? If so, how can you make it better? If you cannot find a way to make it better, no matter how much you market the idea, it will always be second best. First, you need to find a want and need. If you have neither, then you have no market. Once you find the want and need, who is your targeted market? Try your product in other markets too. You'll be surprised at what you may find. When Honda released the Element SUV and marketed it to teens and young adults, they found that it wasn't the young adults buying and driving. Instead, it was the older crowd that found the Honda Element appealing.

Step Two: Your name. Is your name creative? Something memorable is key. Take your business name ideas and create a poll with some of your closest friends and family. Naming is important to the success of your brand or product, but remember, the decision is ultimately yours. If you don't have an emotional connection to it, don't use it.

Step Three: Marketing. Being original is very important when marketing a product or service. Maybe take the product and make it into a song or endorse a local charity or celebrity or restaurant to stand out from the rest of the crowd.

One thing I have done to be creative is, when I come up with something crazy, that I feel is genius, I present the idea to family or customers. If they say, "Hmmm, that might work", it's usually not as good as it could be. When I present an idea and they laugh at how ridiculous it is, I know I am onto something. Remember one thing. When you're onto something big, think bigger. I like to sit down and work out all the kinks, numbers, plans and if it works on paper, I run with it.

Take your business or service and think of ways you can be original.

Building A Business System

Like I mentioned before, your business is like a child. Now, what keeps your child healthy is mainly the systems. The system is the engine that powers and maintains everything.

The business system has many moving parts and each one of those parts must run in unison for the business to work properly. Every business should have its core systems in place and must be followed or the business will fail.

A simple example of a business system is McDonalds. They have simple product, a simple price and are very convenient. However, what's behind the scenes of a McDonalds is one of the most complex business systems in the world. The reason why McDonalds works so well, is that each person has a task to follow. If at any point, the chain is broken, the system will stall. But even then, if each person follows procedure, the company will still operate efficiently.

These rules apply to your business too. Most small business owners are the salesman, the landlord, the accountant, the janitor, stock the warehouse, unload the trucks, place orders, ship orders, etc. Essentially, they created one really big JOB for themselves, not a business. For your business to grow, you'll need to hire people. That means giving up responsibility of some, if not many of the tasks. The problem you run into as a small business owner is that you have or will become a slave of your creation if it is not designed properly. You can do this by building a strong foundation. That foundation starts with getting the right people to handle each task appropriately.

For your new hires to do their jobs properly, you'll need to formulate a system. As you hire more and more people, this system will get more and more complex. For your company to run efficiently and profitable, your employee's responsibilities must be clear to be completed properly.

So, in relation to the body, every organ, every muscle, every cell, every part of our body serves an intricate purpose to ensure the machine runs exactly like it should. None of this would happen if it wasn't for the systems in place.

Expect Good Things

The saying goes you must give to receive. You must give respect to get respect. You must give love to get love. And you must give money if you want something in return. The same goes for your business. If you don't give your business one hundred percent, it won't give it back. My advice to any business owner is to love your business like a child. It's born, it lives, it thrives, and it even makes you proud. It puts a smile on your face. It makes you cry. It's a breathing, living, growing extension of you and someday, like everything in this world, it will die. But, like everything you do, if you love it, cherish it, raise it to be successful, it will love you back.

When your first child was born, what did you expect? You expected good things. You want your child to succeed. You want your child to fall in love. You want your child to someday make a child of their own, move out on their own and care for themselves. That is no different than a business. If the business is raised properly, it will outlive you. If raised properly, someday it will take care of you. If raised properly, it will branch out into other smaller businesses and someday grow into something as strong as its daddy. So, when starting your first business, love it like a child, give it everything it needs and expect good things.

Increase Sales by Properly Training Your Sales People

I see too many sales organizations today pushing for more and more sales people rather than making their current sales people better. It is very expensive for a sales organization to hire new sales people to bring better results and then firing the weaker sales people only after a month or so of poor production. This is honestly like throwing your old TV away because there is nothing to watch, rather than switching cable providers.

There are plenty of sales training classes and seminars out there and from what I have found, these courses are teaching sales people to memorize scripts. This is NOT how you train sales people. Sales really is just thinking on your feet and being great at your craft of problem solving. You cannot teach people a script to solve common problems on the sales floor.

In addition, poor sales performance comes from lack of interest or just being crapped out. I believe that most sales people are really good at their craft but the organization itself is what is harming the sales and performance of the sales people. Poor pay, poor marketing and the organization not having the right focus in mind spins the sales person's mind, impairing their ability to sell.

Sales organizations put fear in sales people and with sales being a mental-based business, the sales person gets in their own head and literally paralyzes their ability to close the deal. Unfortunately, most sales organizations today lack in the uplifting and positive environments and are most focused on their bottom end resulting in cut backs.

Another huge mistake management takes today is overworking their sales people. I see sales people working ten, twelve or more hours each day to hit their quotas. This may seem productive because they are working more hours, but the mental fatigue ultimately is making a lot of those hours useless also causing them to resent their jobs. Management can properly train and encourage their sales teams to get the results they would expect, allowing the sales people to work less hours, enjoy their jobs, spend time with their families and giving the organization less turnover.

The solutions to these problems are out there. Why don't they just pay attention? I'll explain in another book, but the answer is simple, times have changed, the game has changed, and they want to play by the old rules.

Happiness

I have heard money doesn't bring happiness. Neither does being broke or poor? Do you know the difference between being broke and poor? Poor people are poor forever. They are born poor and die poor. Broke people have money either put away that they refuse to spend, or an event has happened making it difficult for them to keep that money. Being poor is eternal. Being broke is temporary. Use these tools in this book to build your financial outlook. Its ok to be broke, because it means you are hungry, you are eager to build wealth and want to work hard to get to that goal of achievement. Do what you feel is right in your life, but make sure your attention isn't spent on spending because you're sad or depressed, but spending to make you a happier person.

Referring back to purses. You hate your job. Your life is so drab. When you're sad, don't go out and buy a purse. Instead, build a business to get you out of that dead-end job and sell those very same purses to others to build your wealth and health.

Conclusion

I think the most important part of building a business is staying Green. If you're not Green, meaning eager to learn and grow, you're dead. Get out of the business and move on. For over 20 years, I have build successful and unsuccessful business, but that's what entrepreneurship is all about. We come up with ideas and try them. Sometimes we do well. Sometimes we fail. But with every success and failure is a lesson. Nobody ever said education wasn't cheap. Some people go to college and get a degree and find a job. Others, like myself, never went to college. We just dabbled in this or that until something worked and stuck with it until it didn't work anymore, then went onto something else. Essentially, that's all business is.

Enjoy being an entrepreneur. Learn. Grow. Adapt. Innovate. And as my father always told me, use your head not your back. It's quicker to get it done right the first time, than having to do it twice.

Other Titles by Jon Robert Quinn

Books

- Being Quinnessential: Beginners Guide to Becoming a Gentleman (2018)

- Searching for Sara (2017)

- Tips to Increase Your Wealth, Health & Life (2009)

Music

- New Faces (2000)
- Solo-Fisticated (2004)
- One Long Road (2004)
- JeRQ THIS (2005)
- Live '05 (2005)
- JeRQ THIS TOO (2006)
- The Road to Hammerlane (2006)
- A New Beginning (2007)
- The Best of Jon Robert Quinn (2008)
- One Day at a Time (2009)
- JeRQ THIS 3 (2010)
- 1982 (2015)
- The Best of Jon Robert Quinn: Vol 2 (2016)
- Made in England (2017)
- Quinnessential: 20 Years (2018)

Talk Shows

- The Good Life Show with Jon Robert Quinn (2015)
- 60 Minute Success (2016)
- The Cash Cow Show (2017)
- Why Pay Six Percent Show (2017)
- Investor Profits Now (2017)
- Real Estate Investor Weekly (2017)
- Women's Wealth Warrior Show (2018)
- The Jon Robert Quinn Show (2018)
- The Everyday CFO (2018)
- The Body by Vlad Show (2018)
- License to Kill (2018)
- Your Perfect Home (2018)
- Get Detoxinated (2018)

www.ingramcontent.com/pod-product-compliance
Lightning Source LLC
Chambersburg PA
CBHW031557210526
45464CB00003B/1325